Thoughts of Consequence

Kayte Ray

Presentation by *BookLeaf Publishing*

Web: www.bookleafpub.com

E-mail: info@bookleafpub.com

ISBN: 9789357441001

First edition 2023

To my Family-

*Thank you for giving me the room to grow
as a person and a writer.*

*Thank you to all the wonderful writers on
fanstory.com for all your support and
encouragement.*

ACKNOWLEDGEMENT

JMM- Thanks for all your support and encouragement

The Poet

Line by line,
the story rises in me like a wave.
Lost in time,
I scribble words onto the page.
Hope to find
the true great wisdom of the sage.
as line by line
I put my secrets all away
and lost in time,
the words, I find, now flow like the rain.
Hope to find
the deepest secrets of the age
as line by line
I put my story to the page.

Confession

Soft Spoken
The words flow like honey, thick and dauntless
Slowly moving through open air, unstoppable
clinging to every surface hot molasses,
sticky and unforgiving.
They spill the truth like hot tea
rushing over shaking hands
Burning ever so slightly as they pass.
Speak carefully,
for they only fly one way.
They ride the air
like the fresh aroma
of home made bread
sensed, unseen
unavoidable.
Making their presence known
to everyone they pass
with their implacable truth.

Change

Rush in
Hold on
Stay strong
Be not afraid.
Watch as the walls come down.
Hold fast
Keep on
Believe
Stand your ground.
(and) watch as the walls come down.
Let go
Breathe in
Release
Keep the faith.
Rest in the truth you've found.
Stand tall
Be still
Find peace
Know your place
(and) watch as the walls come down.

Inspiration

Shaking ever so silently
as the words don't come,
put pen to paper tirelessly
waiting for inspiration.

Will it strike
Like a fast moving car?
Like a torrent of flood?
 Will it stop me in my tracks
with unavoidable vigor?

Standing still as to not disturb its flow
I wait

Untitled

5

Set it up and knock it down,
another day gone by..
The truth of it is on the wind,
it matters not to try
to see these things the way you should,
that presence in the sky,
just set it up and knock it down
another day gone by.

Breathe

Smell the pipe tobacco's scent
Floating on the air.
It lifts and curls in the smoke
Until there's nothing there.
Hints of berry on the vine
Tastes of sugar and red wine
Such a sweetness, well defined
You breathe it in most every time.

Untitled

Honesty
Falling fresh on
Clarity
The human race is
Meant to be
The keeper of the flame.

Truth
cannot be seen
as optional
standing in the shade of all
the world has to say.

Countenance
falling fresh on
Brilliance
When lies pass
as a sufferance
The future ends today.

Hold On

Rest in the chill of the morning
Let go of the darkness of night
Hold fast to mercy and wisdom
Praise to the birth of the light.
Hold on
Pray in the edge of the daytime
Lay down your worry and care
Let not your spirit be troubled
Creation has met you right there
Hold on
Wake to the beauty around you
Our world refreshed in the rite
The grace of the living surrounds you
Exhale the breath of the night.
Hold on
Hail Apollo the sunlight
The secret of ages anew
Time past a present around you
Your soul in the waking Renewed
Hold on
Rest in the chill of the morning
Let go of the darkness of night
Hold fast to mercy and wisdom
Praise to the birth of the light

Daylight and Darkness

9

Breathe in the beauty
of the sun not yet risen
The darkness of night before day.
Bask in the sunrise
as daylight and moon glow
switch places beginning the day.

watch as shadows give
way to the to the daylight
as all nature awakens to play

Watch as the daylight
now chasing the shadows
is keeping the darkness at bay.

CHRISTINE (a look at ALS)

I watched your body crumble
there was nothing I could do
the sickness took up residence
deep inside of you

That day I was a child
the wish I made was true
The Gods must have been listening
to what I wished for you

The sun shone bright that autumn day
the sky was clear and blue
I asked if they would take you home
if better wouldn't do

The Gods stepped in
and on that day
your body met its end
and you were free from suffering
and moving once again.

Sunrise

Watch the sun ease out over the horizon
as the Fire Gods paint an intangible display
of the perfection of flame across the dawning
sky.
Soak in the beauty as the splendor of morning
light
fades into the coming of day.
 Nestle into a hot cup of coffee like a warm
blanket
and the energy of a loved one like a soft breeze
(ever so gently stealing your breath for just a
moment)
Be not afraid.
Sink into the day, eyes open,
unbroken, what (but good)
 could follow such perfection?

Whispers

Fear not oh World
with your darkened feats of consciousness
ride the silver mists of insecurity
long into the bleak night air and
rest my tortured soul.

To reason with the demons of injustice
I call upon your sanity
Lengthen my stay
and with your quiet voice
speak my name
Not demanding only hoping I'll respond.

New Day

Take in the light of a new day
waiting in the silence
as the first rays of light
dance off the dew laden grass.
Breathe in the chill of the air
Let it fill your lungs with
cool crystaline comfort
as the sun rises.
Rest in the stillness around you
As the first birds sing
welcoming the day
in all its splendor
Wake, as the beauty surrounds you
standing alone in the dawning light
as the darkness fades,
and the new day greets you
Strong and stoic
Complete and
Quiet

Forgiveness Prayer

People make mistakes
There is nothing to be done
I never meant to hurt you
I was sure you were the one

Now years have passed
And in our way
A friendship has begun
With stronger roots
In firmer ground
Than the love we spun

That love is there still
In its way
Making sure we don't betray
This new beginning
So please stay

Have a sip of tea with me
People make mistakes you see
If this is all that we will be
Let it be the best of me.

Fly

Soar in the edge of the evening
on wings of silver and gold
remember you rise from the ashes
the flame having nourished your soul.

See the face of God in the first light of the
morning
The spirit of creation in the tides.
See the love of all the living in the light of a new
day
The strength of the family in the sunrise

Dance on the edge of the daylight
Holding your hope firm in hand
Know that the love will surround you
No matter the place where you stand.

Listen

Listen as the rainfall
breaks the silence of a new day.
Listen as the wind
whispers its truth.
Watch as the fire Gods
embrace the fresh morning
in the sunrise that slowly surrounds you

Feel the water gods
 inhabit the dew
Lying fresh on the grass 'neath your feet
Rest in the stillness
 of the world around you
hold back nothing
be all you can be.

Carry On

17

Stand on the edge of tomorrow
know that your future is bright
have faith in the world around you
never give up on the fight.
Know that today you are given
the past is now buried and gone
Find peace in the truth of the moment
Know that you must carry on

Morning Breath

Inhale
The robust aroma of fresh coffee
Dancing on the air like a feather in the wind
Ever lifted and carried along on the breeze
The smell of morning.
Taste the hardy bitterness
as it dances across your tongue
Strong, sturdy, unshakable
Like the loving embrace of family
Holding steady at its pace, undiminished.
Relax as its heat warms you
Slowly flowing through your system
sultry like honey
sticking to every surface as it passes.
Allow the breath to leave you
The emptiness resting heavy on your lungs
Like the firm embrace of family
allow the heaviness to engulf you
Breathing in again.

Love

So close
I feel your skin on my skin
So close
I feel your heart beat as mine
I feel your temperature rise
as you hold me
I feel your mind slow
if only for a moment
The world disappears
in the presence of it all
I feel your breath slow
as I kiss you
Your embrace tighten and
for just this moment
there is only
you and I

Dusk

As crickets sing their mournful song
In welcome of the night
The evening sky
with purpose on
brings closure to the light.

Truth

Be careful with your truth my dear
you know not how it hurts.
Speak softly with conviction here
Your words have weight and berth

Be honest with an open mind
the words are yours to share
But know that they are just like time
floating on the air

You cannot take the meaning back
Once it is released.
The pain you cause with present fact
Brings nothing close to peace.